A Christian Sermon on God's Foreknowledge or Election to Salvation

From the Gospel of Matthew, Chapter 22

Delivered in the Royal Chapel at Wolffenbüttel

by Dr. Martin Chemnitz

on the 20th Sunday after Trinity

Published in 1573

Translated by Paul A. Rydecki

Repristination Press
Malone, Texas

A translation *Eine Predigt uber das Evangelion Matth. 22. Von dem König der seinem Sohn Hochzeit machet etc. Dahin der hohe Artickel von der Versehung Gottes auffs aller einfeltigest erkleret wird* by Martin Chemnitz. Copyright 2016 by Paul A. Rydecki. Published by permission of the translator. No part of this publication may be reproduced, stored in a retrieval system, or transmitted in any form or by any means, electronic, mechanical, photocopying or otherwise without the prior written permission of Repristination Press.

Scripture taken from the New King James Version. Copyright © 1982 by Thomas Nelson, Inc. Used by permission. All rights reserved.

ISBN 1-891469-73-8
Published in 2016.

REPRISTINATION PRESS
P.O. BOX 173
BYNUM, TEXAS 76631

www.repristinationpress.com

And Jesus answered and spoke to them again by parables and said: "The kingdom of heaven is like a certain king who arranged a marriage for his son, and sent out his servants to call those who were invited to the wedding; and they were not willing to come. Again, he sent out other servants, saying, 'Tell those who are invited, "See, I have prepared my dinner; my oxen and fatted cattle are killed, and all things are ready. Come to the wedding."' But they made light of it and went their ways, one to his own farm, another to his business. And the rest seized his servants, treated them spitefully, and killed them. But when the king heard about it, he was furious. And he sent out his armies, destroyed those murderers, and burned up their city. Then he said to his servants, 'The wedding is ready, but those who were invited were not worthy. Therefore go into the highways, and as many as you find, invite to the wedding.' So those servants went out into the highways and gathered together all whom they found, both bad and good. And the wedding hall was filled with guests. But when the king came in to see the guests, he saw a man there who did not have on a wedding garment. So he said to him, 'Friend, how did you come in here without a wedding garment?' And he was speechless. Then the king said to the servants, 'Bind him hand and foot, take him away, and cast him into outer darkness; there will be weeping and gnashing of teeth.' For many are called, but few are chosen." (NKJV)

In the Gospel for today which was read earlier, we have a parable about a King who arranged a wedding for His Son and about how things went for Him with the invited guests, etc. Now, it is the nature of a parable that one must seek to understand from it something other than what the words declare. But this may immediately prompt the question, "Does that mean that each one may interpret this parable however he wishes? Can one person interpret it one way and another interpret it differently, as each one sees fit?" St. Peter gives the answer in 2 Pet. 1: No! For the prophecy of Scripture does not depend on anyone's private interpretation, as if our Lord God had given the text only to us and had left the interpretation or explanation open to our whim. No, the commandments of the Lord are not only clear to Him, but they also enlighten our dark eyes, as David says in Psalm 19. Therefore, Christ always sets forth with clear, precise words, either at the beginning or at the end, how He wants His parables to be understood, even as He states the conclusion at the end of this parable: "For many are called, but few are chosen." With these words, it is as if He were pointing with His finger, showing us how we are to explain, understand, and use the parable in today's Gospel. Namely, that in it is contained and revealed the difficult article concerning the lofty mystery of God's foreknowledge—how God foreknew, elected, and predestined the elect in Christ Jesus to eternal life. For since this article is a great mystery concerning which human reason can easily and quickly go astray, and nevertheless is a doctrine that is important for simple Christians to know about—a very useful and comforting doctrine—Christ summarized this lofty article about the great mystery of God's foreknowledge in a common, simple parable, so that preachers, first of all, might thereby be reminded that they should not go too deeply into this article, and also so that the hearers should keep their thoughts concerning this article in check, lest they stray from the simplicity of the parable in today's Gospel. For this is what gave the Lord Christ occasion to tell this parable: In the previous chapter, when He had threatened the Jewish people with God's judgment and wrath on account of their despising of the Gospel, they made the following appeal: "Are we not God's chosen people? Surely God's election and foreknowledge cannot fail! How, then, can we be rejected, even if we despise Christ and His Gospel?" Christ answers with this parable in which He demonstrates in a simple way the true understanding and the right use of the doctrine of God's foreknowledge and election.

Thus we have from the Lord Christ Himself what the explanation of this parable is and should be. Namely, that the doctrine concerning the true understanding and the right use of the article of God's foreknowledge and election is revealed therein. The Holy Spirit has also taught us about this in the Scriptures, where we see what sort of teaching is founded on each passage in the Scripture—how we may handle, understand, and use it in a fruitful, beneficial, and salutary manner. Namely, as Paul says in Rom. 15: "Everything that was written was written to teach us, in order that, through patience and comfort, we might have hope." And in 1 Cor. 10: "It was written as a warning for us." 2 Tim. 3: "All Scripture inspired by God is useful for instruction, reproof, admonition and correction." Thus our dear God has chosen to preserve us in a faithful and fatherly way, so that we may know how we are to conduct ourselves with His Word, in order that we may indeed be found on the path that He Himself has shown us and pointed out to us in the Scriptures. And if we handle His Word and hear it in this way, we will be strong and will have the comfort that He wants to work in us through it by His Spirit. For the Word of God, when it is preached, heard, and meditated upon, is an office of the Holy Spirit (2 Cor. 3), and the living seed through which we are born again (1 Pet. 1). Indeed, it is the power of God that saves all who believe it (Rom. 1).

According to this Scriptural model, we will now, in the simplest way possible, deal with these three parts from today's Gospel: First, how the doctrine of the lofty article of God's foreknowledge or election is expressed so simply, basically, and clearly by the Lord Christ in this parable; in what this foreknowledge or election of God consists and upon what it is based. Secondly, how this doctrine serves as a warning, reproof, admonition, and correction for us if we should despise or refuse God's call or oppose it with blasphemies and persecutions. Thirdly, what sweet comfort this doctrine affords, that God, in His counsel, predestined us to eternal salvation, and considered even before the foundation of the world was laid the means by which He would bring us there. May the faithful and true God give us His Spirit and grace, so that such hearing may benefit and prosper us for instruction, admonition, and comfort. Amen.

Part 1

It is certain and clear from God's Word that all those who are to inherit eternal life were foreknown, elected, and predestined to that end by God before the foundation of the world was laid. For this is what Paul says in Eph. 1: "God the Father has blessed us with every kind of spiritual blessing through Christ, even as He chose us in Him before the foundation of the world was laid." And in 2 Tim. 1: "Grace was given us according to God's purpose in Christ Jesus before the time of the world." In John 13, Christ says: "I am not speaking about all of you. I know whom I have chosen." Romans 9: "In order that the purpose of God might stand according to election, it was said, not by the merit of works but by the grace of the One who called, 'The older shall serve the younger.'" Romans 8: "Those whom He previously foreknew, them He also predestined that they should conform to the likeness of His Son." 2 Tim. 2: "The solid foundation of God stands, having this seal: The Lord knows His own." Phi. 4: "Whose names are written in the Book of Life," and other similar passages in the Scriptures.

But in this article, human reason can quickly and easily reach too far or climb too high. For since God's foreknowledge can neither fail nor be changed (Rom. 11, Isa.

46), the mischievous world takes advantage of this and is confirmed thereby in its own security and wickedness. "If I am predestined for salvation, then I cannot fail to reach it, whether or not I despise Word and Sacrament or trouble myself to believe with repentance or to amend my life." On the other hand, the troubled, bad conscience often enters into the following struggle: "Who knows if your name, too, is recorded in the Book of Life, even if you hold fast to the Word, even if, by God's grace, you are penitent and believing and have begun to live a new life? But if your name was not recorded in the Book of Life before the beginning of the world, it is all in vain and for nothing. For others, too, have made such a beginning and nevertheless have finally fallen away, etc." For this reason, some have determined that one should not preach anything at all to the Christians in the Church about God's foreknowledge and election, since, as stated, there is danger on both sides, either to fall into security or into doubt. But since our dear God has revealed this doctrine to us on many occasions and in many passages of the Scriptures, we must not sweep it under the rug. Neither can nor should we say that it is useless, offensive, or harmful, as long as we see to it that we do not reach too far or climb too high into it. Rather, we must grasp and retain the true understanding and the right use of it in all simplicity.

Indeed, the Lord Christ shows us in this parable how this can be done in the simplest possible way. For, as is His custom, when He has a point of doctrine to teach us that is hard for us to grasp, He puts it in the form of a parable so that not only the highly gifted and learned, but also the simple, the young, and the childlike may, by God's grace, understand and grasp from His teaching as much as they need to know for their salvation. So, then, since He well knows how lofty this article of God's foreknowledge is and how easily a human heart can go astray in it, He has, for the good of us poor little children, put this lofty mystery into a simple parable, in order that we may have from it a good, clear account—as much as is useful and necessary for us for instruction, admonition, and comfort. Not only has He summed up this great mystery in a simple parable, but He has also chosen to give and to set a certain limit and boundary so that we do not indulge our thoughts too deeply in this article. But when we wish to run too far with it or climb too high into it, we are to place our finger over our mouth with the dear apostle Paul and say: "Oh, the depth of the riches, both of the wisdom and knowledge of God! How incomprehensible are His judgments, and His ways beyond finding out!" Indeed, when the simple-minded read, hear, discuss or think about this article of God's foreknowledge, there is no better or surer way for them than that they always keep this parable before their eyes and in their hearts, gathering up all the disputes concerning this article and placing them into a chest together with the parable's simplicity. And then, if the thoughts that Christ Himself has set forth in this parable would run too far or climb too high outside of that chest, then we should always think in this way: For this very reason my dear Lord Christ has summed up this lofty article in a parable, so that I might remain in its simplicity and know how far and wide I should go in this article. And with regard to whatever is asked or disputed that goes above and beyond the simplicity of this parable, I say this: "That is neither useful nor necessary for me to investigate. I will remain with this article in the chest in which the Lord Christ Himself, for the sake of my simplemindedness, has placed the doctrine in this parable. Whatever lies beyond that belongs in the abyss of God's wisdom. I have no business delving into this. I will stick with this parable and give thanks to my dear Lord Christ that He has summed up this lofty article in such a simple story. And if I stick with it, I know that I can neither err nor go astray. On the contrary, I will know and have as much from this article as I need to know from it in this life for salvation."

So, then, this parable shows us in what the article of God's foreknowledge consists and on what it stands. For otherwise, human reason would depict this article in an absolute sense, imagining that God's foreknowledge and election consist in the following: Since all future events stand in the present for our Lord God, He held a sort of muster before the world began and said concerning one person, "Write this one's name in the Book of Life," and concerning another, "Write this one's name in the Book of Death. This one will be saved; that one will be rejected and damned." As Gerson* writes, "They imagine that God had some such

---

* Jean Gerson (1363–1429), Chancellor of the University of Paris, is often cited by Lutheran theologians as a reformer.

imaginations, as if a master chef had a farm full of chickens, and he ordered the cook, 'Cut off this one's head, let that one go free, etc.'" Indeed, when a person indulges in such thoughts, the whole article is confused and tangled up.

But in this parable the Lord Christ shows, point by point, what all belongs to this article and how one point always follows from and after the other. Namely, that God's foreknowledge or election stands on and consists in this, that our dear God saw beforehand that the human race would fall away from Him through sin and would thereby sink under God's wrath and the devil's power into eternal destruction and condemnation; that our dear God, before the foundation of the world was laid, considered, determined, and concluded in His secret divine counsel how the human race might be rescued from its destruction and brought again to salvation. Namely, that, first, His only Son would take on human nature, that is, as the parable says, that the King would make a wedding for His Son and wed Him to the human nature. Secondly, that He should be made under the Law and be slaughtered as a guilt offering for our sin, and thus, through Him, all that is necessary for this joyful wedding of eternal salvation would be prepared. Thirdly, that for this salvation, He would have not only the flesh and blood that His dear Son would assume in the unity of His person, but also other guests, too, not from among the fallen angels, but from the human race, which, on account of the assumed human nature, has been befriended and endeared to the Son of God as His Bride, flesh of His flesh and bone of His bone. Fourthly, that He would cause these guests of His to be invited to the wedding through His servants, that is, He would reveal this secret counsel of His to the world through the Word, and He would call men to His kingdom through the spoken Word. Fifthly, that, through this call of His, He would be effective and work in the hearts of men, enlighten them, convert and justify them. Sixthly, that those whom He would thus justify, He would also guard, protect, preserve, eternally save, and glorify, as Paul thus binds these pieces together one after another in the beautiful passage in Romans 8, like links in a golden chain. He says, "Those whom God foreknew or predestined, them He also called. Those whom He called, them He also justified. But those whom He justified, them He also glorified." Seventhly, since God saw beforehand that the wickedness of human nature would not heed this call and this working of God but would resist it and would not receive the grace of God when it wants to work in man, He concluded in His purpose that all those who would despise, blaspheme, persecute, or fail to follow Him when He wants to work in them by His grace and would persist in such resistance, should be punished here temporally, and be eternally rejected and condemned, as this parable clearly demonstrates.

This is the simple understanding and meaning as to what pertains to the foreknowledge of God, in what it consists, and on what it is based. We should keep all these pieces together whenever we speak or think about God's foreknowledge or election, as Paul handles and reveals this doctrine piece by piece throughout the entire first chapter of Ephesians. For if I remain with the account in its simplicity, then I have as much as I need to know about this doctrine, and I know that I cannot err or go astray. But if someone here wants to continue arguing, "But God certainly knows beforehand who and how many will receive this call of His through grace and who will resist it!" —to him I reply, "God undoubtedly knows that and much more. But I have not been commanded to delve into it. Instead, I will remain with the simplicity of this parable." Likewise, if someone were to ask, "Since these two pieces are inseparable, that those who were elected were also called, why, then, does God not send His Word—through which the call takes place—purely and unadulterated into every land?" Here I reply: "My parable, in which the Lord Christ has summed up this doctrine for me, does not extend that far. Therefore, in this question, I will join Paul in Rom. 9 and Isa. 45 and place a finger over my mouth and say, 'Oh, the depth of the wisdom of God, etc.' Now, I recognize God's righteous wrath toward those who do not have God's Word—which we would all merit and deserve together with them. But to me and to others who are called, I recognize God's pure grace, apart from—indeed, contrary to—all our merit, and I heartily thank Him for it. I cannot go beyond that, nor do I desire to go any higher. Rather, I will remain inside the confines of this simple parable, in order that I may neither run too far nor climb too high.

If others have greater gifts, so that they can reach higher into this article, I wish them well. But since my dear Lord Christ has comprehended this great mystery in a simple parable—and not without good reason—I will stick with the proverb of Solomon: *Qui simpliciter ambulat, bene ambulat.* He who walks simply walks most securely."

Thus this parable shows us, first, the true explanation and right understanding of the doctrine concerning God's foreknowledge and election. But the doctrine is enshrined in this parable in such a way that each part—indeed, practically every word—contains in itself such beautiful doctrine and glorious comfort that this whole parable deserves for all the words and parts of it to be diligently treated and considered. We will now briefly offer pious Christians a brief introduction to this.

With regard to Christ's incarnation and what pertains to it and follows from it, we see it beautifully and comfortingly depicted in the parable when He says, "The King (God the Father) makes a wedding for His Son." That is, He marries to Him a bride. Now, the Christian Church is, in a different context, referred to as the Bride of the Lord Christ (Eph. 5, Hos. 2). But since in this parable the bride and the guests are referred to separately, with the elect being signified by the guests, the bride in this parable is properly understood to be the human nature that was united with the Son of God in the unity of His person. Now, according to the nature and particular imagery of the parable, a bride is placed, by virtue of the marriage, in communion with the honor, dignity, and property of the bridegroom. Therefore, in this world and in this life, each one carefully seeks a wife who is fit for him, who is apt and worthy of his honor. But since this heavenly King wants to make a wedding for His Son, what kind of bride will He find for Him? Nothing either in heaven or on earth is comparable to Him or fit for Him, so He also does not receive the angelic nature (Heb. 2), but Abraham's seed, that is, human nature, and that not before, but after the Fall. "But what is man that You think of him, and the son of man that You receive him?" says David in Psalm 8. To be sure, this human nature is not only earth, as Adam says, nor only dust and ashes, as Abraham says, but it is corrupted by sin and fallen away from God. Indeed, it has become God's enemy (Rom. 8). It lies now under the power of Satan, like a fiery brand, condemned by God's judgment to eternal flames. And should now the lofty divine majesty wed and marry this human nature to His only Son? Surely it could never happen, if it depended on our worthiness. But here God praises His unfathomable, indescribable love, grace, and mercy, in that His only Son receives this poor human nature, not merely as a slave or a servant, but He weds it to Himself as a bride, and thus not only snatches it out from under Satan's power, but exalts it and sets it above all angels and over whatever high, great, mighty, and glorious thing that can be named, not only in this world, but also in the world to come (Eph. 1). Not that the human nature became equal to the Godhead, but that, through the personal union, it was placed in communion with the honor, dignity, and property of the Son of God and, after the state of humiliation, was openly exalted to it, as this doctrine is expressly treated elsewhere. This is a glorious pledge of our redemption and salvation, that the human nature, which Satan had torn so far away from God through sin, is now again so intimately and essentially united with God that, from now on, to the entire person of the Son of God there belongs not only His divine nature, but also our human nature which was received by Him; and that He wishes to accomplish the work of our salvation not only by His divine nature, but also by the human nature that He has received, according to which He is our Brother, and we are flesh of His flesh. The prophet Ezekiel describes in chapter 16 what tremendous grace this is. He holds up the divine majesty and our human nature next to each other, having found the latter in impurity, wretchedness, and poverty, and yet not only consoled it, but personally united Himself with it by His conception of the Holy Spirit. When a godly heart ponders this great mystery in this way, the parable offers glorious comfort and presents a doctrine that is even more beautiful.

Perhaps you will say that, yes, the flesh and blood are indeed blessed which have been united with the Son of God in the unity of His person, but how are the rest of us helped by this? This parable answers that question: We are guests whom the King wants to invite and have present at the wedding celebration of His Son. Now, one takes care to invite to a wedding those who have been befriended by the bridegroom and bride and are related to them. And therefore the fallen angels do not come to this wedding celebration, for this Bridegroom has not taken upon Himself the angelic nature (Heb. 2). But since the Bridegroom is our Brother according to His received human nature and we are related to Him as flesh of His flesh and bone of His bone, we men become, by grace, the invited guests at this wedding.

But, you say, there is a big difference here. The flesh of the Son of God was conceived by the Holy Spirit and knows nothing of sin. In our flesh, on the other hand, dwells nothing good. On the contrary, it is a body of sins and of death, as Paul says. How, then, are we to share in this wedding celebration?

The parable provides the answer to this question. The Bridegroom humbled Himself. He set aside His glory for a while. He was made under the Law and was slaughtered for our sin in order that He, all by Himself, might prepare whatever is necessary for us to attend this wedding celebration and earn for us the privilege of being wedding guests who share in the celebration. All of these are beautiful, blessed, comforting thoughts.

It is likewise beautiful and lovely that the preaching of the Gospel is described in the parable in this way: The King sent forth His servants to call the guests to the wedding. Thus when preachers preach repentance and the forgiveness of sins, they are nothing else but the wedding heralds of our Lord God, through whom He calls us to the wedding celebration of eternal salvation. And Paul indeed praises it as a special grace of God that our dear God reveals and makes known to us His mysterious, hidden counsel (which is otherwise a mystery that is hidden from the whole world, as Paul says) through the preaching of the Gospel. If I want to know what God, in grace, concluded concerning my salvation, I ought not to climb up into heaven, which is too high for me, but I can be informed of this through the call that is brought before me in the preaching of the Gospel and that is sealed and confirmed through the Sacraments. For I should by no means imagine that, if my dear God has called me by His Word to salvation, He actually intends something else. For He is a faithful God and His heart is true. Rather, we should think and judge concerning His heart, will, and mind based on and according to His Word, as Paul says in 1 Corinthians 2. We have and know the heart and mind of Christ. In order to prove that it is this King's sincere and earnest desire to have these guests present, He says in the parable that "the King was angry when they were not willing to come." In addition, we know that the very call that goes out through the Word is the only established means by which the Holy Spirit wants to be effective in us and work in our hearts to enlighten, convert, and justify us, so that, being reconciled through God's grace for Christ's sake, we may become heirs of eternal life, whom He wishes to guard in His hand, preserve until the end, and bless with eternal glory, as the same doctrine is presented in Romans 8 and in other passages of Scripture. We will explore this a bit more in the third part. For now, we have wanted merely to offer a brief introduction and explain how the Word in this parable may be weighed and considered usefully, beneficially, and for one's consolation.

Let this suffice for a brief review of the first part, how the doctrine of the article on the foreknowledge or election of God is presented simply in this parable, and how a Christian can ponder this article according to this parable in a simple, edifying way.

20

Part 2

The second part of the sermon, as noted at the beginning, will deal with this: how we ought to use and benefit from the doctrine of God's foreknowledge or election as it has now been presented and explained, for admonition, reproof, admonition, and correction. For it is both useful and necessary that we have the proper understanding of this oft-presented doctrine. It is not, however, enough that we remain content with knowing it, understanding it, and being able to speak about it and discuss it. No, we must always consider how we should benefit from this doctrine and to what end we should use it.

Now, comfort is surely the chief part. But this parable is chiefly intended to serve as a warning, reproof, admonition, and correction. Therefore, we will, secondly, treat this part, according to the text of the parable, for the purpose of correction, and in the third part we will speak about its comfort.

For the Jews, against all admonition, were living under the delusion that, "We are surely the elect people of God. We have His Word, too," which, in this parable, is referred to as the call. "And even if we don't follow the Word, or if we blaspheme and persecute Christ and the apostles, since we bear the title and boast that we are called the people of God," that is, the guests of this King, as the parable states, "none of this can be taken away from us. We are still God's children and heirs of eternal salvation." But as John the Baptist says to the Pharisees in Matthew 3, "Do not imagine that you can say to yourselves, 'We have Abraham as our father.' I say to you, God is able to raise up children to Abraham from these stones." Paul refutes this same delusion with a powerful argument in Romans 9. Thus also the Lord Christ sets up this parable against the same stubborn delusion in such a simple, clear and basic manner that the Pharisees themselves realize that He is talking about them, says Matthew. Namely, when God the heavenly King, in His divine counsel before the beginning of the world, predestined or concluded His foreknowledge or election, He did not do it in such a way that the guests—even if they despised the Word by which they were called to this wedding, failed to follow it, mocked and killed His servants, or merely adopted an external appearance and name, without true repentance and conversion—would nonetheless be saved, that is, become participants in this wedding celebration; but only the elect who hear the Word by which they are called, receive it by God's power and blessing, follow it, put off the Old Man through true repentance, and put on the Lord Christ through true faith; who thereafter also allow themselves to be ruled by the Holy Spirit and walk in God's ways—these He will also preserve and eternally save, as described at length in Romans 8 and Ephesians 1. And since God wishes to work this in them through the Word by which He calls them, He has also determined in

His counsel of eternal foreknowledge that, if they themselves resist the working of the Holy Spirit and hinder His working, the guests would not be worthy of it; that is, those who despise the Word when they are called, do not follow it, mistreat and kill His servants, and only rely on outward appearance and remain in this state—that these should not be saved, but be punished here in time and rejected and condemned there in eternal darkness. And He shows this to them piece by piece in this parable and concludes it with this saying: "Many are called, but few are chosen." And Paul says in 2 Timothy 2, "God knows those who are His, and let whoever names the name of Christ turn from iniquity."

Now, if this delusion only existed among the Jews and there were no one among us who deceived himself with similar thoughts, then we would only need to speak here about the Jews and scold them for the same. But the very same thing that happened among the Jews at that time is also in full swing among us Gentiles, as the Lord Christ also sets forth in the parable how the world behaves toward His Word and call, at all times and in all places, first among the Jews, and then also as He sends His servants into the streets, that is, among the Gentiles. Namely, they were not willing to come. Some despised it and mistreated and killed the servants. Others come only for the outward appearance and do not wear the wedding garment, etc. Therefore, this is a common warning and admonition that is just as necessary for us Gentiles who have become His Christians as it was at that time for the Jews. For we know the art so well that we can use it to our advantage and think, "Surely we have God's Word. Surely we profess the Gospel. Surely Christ has earned salvation for us. And even though we otherwise despise both Word and Sacrament, fail to follow the Holy Spirit, mistreat and kill the ministers of Christ, bear only an outward appearance without true repentance and conversion, we will nevertheless be saved." But in order that we should not be led astray with such false imaginations and vain words, we should accustom ourselves always to consider this parable and thereby tear this false delusion from our hearts, so that we are never forced to hear on account of it, "My friend, how did you get in here, etc.?"

Indeed, that is the common explanation of this second part, as the parable expressly demonstrates it. But we must and we shall consider each part in somewhat greater detail. In this way, the warning and admonition will be better sharpened for us.

For the Lord Christ tells this parable as if it were a mournful complaint, because the heavenly King spent so much on this banquet, even slaughtering His only Son, so that He might prepare everything that is necessary and that belongs to the marriage celebration. But when He sends out His servants and orders them to tell the guests, "Behold, everything is ready. Come to the wedding!," it turns out, as the parable says, that they were not willing to come. They despised His invitation and went away, one here, the other there. Some mistreated and killed His servants, etc.

Now, it is a truly remarkable thing that the world excludes itself from this wedding, as the parable says, and refuses to come. For, does our Lord God wish to torture, torment, and kill them? No! He wants to give them eternal life! But, perhaps they have to perform some difficult task at the wedding, like hauling bricks or giving away much or earning much? No, not that, either. For He says, "All is ready. Come to the wedding!" Will they have to hide under the table or chase the dogs out? Is that the reason they won't come? No, He wants to seat them at the high table of His grace, eternal salvation, and glory. But here we see just how miserably human nature has been corrupted by sin, so that it will not allow itself to be helped. When God says, "Come to the wedding!," as the parable says, they will not come.

What other reason could there be? In other cases, all men would happily be saved, and everyone seeks his own well-being. But when our Lord God says, "Come to My wedding!"—that is, "I wish to save you!"—and they are not willing to come, why does it always turn out this way? We can easily find the answer in this parable. For the invitation to this wedding does not say, "Remain in your sins without repentance! Remain as you are and go forth without amending your lives! You will still be saved!" No, on the contrary, it means, "Repent!" For whoever comes to the wedding, as the invitation says, must not remain where he is. The world prefers darkness to light. They will not come to the wedding if it means they have to abandon their evil deeds. "If I were a false spirit," says Micah in chapter 2, "and preached how they might drink and overindulge," fornicate and binge, skimp, mistreat, mock, lie, and commit other forms of mischief, and nevertheless be saved, "that would be a preacher for this people!," says the prophet. But since God's Word does not permit these things, but rather admonishes, reproves, and cries out, "Repent!" this is why some say that they will not come. Some people let our Lord God continue to rebuke them through the Law while they continue to go wherever and do whatever their evil desire bids and drives them.

But what causes some people to mistreat and kill His servants, since they are messengers sent to proclaim peace and salvation (Isa. 52)? Answer: The Holy Spirit must rebuke the world and will not allow their wicked behavior to go unpunished. But the world cannot bear this, as Hosea says in chapter 4: "Let no one contend with nor reprove anyone, for Your people are like those who contend with the priests themselves." If only this King would command His servants to stop reproving "in season and out of season"! That is the reason why it follows, as the parable says, that "some seized His servants, mistreated and killed them." It also happens, as the parable demonstrates, because the servants have a certain, solemn command to call the guests in this way: "Behold, all is ready. Come to the wedding!" But the world wants to weave its own works, merit, and holiness into the article of justification before God and include these things in its salvation. Since the servants of this King refuse to teach like the people want them to, the people either will not come, or they mistreat and kill the servants. This is another point that the parable makes. If the wedding were arranged around the outward appearance and names of the guests, then the world would indeed send many guests to this wedding. But since, in Christ, there is to be a genuine, truthful way of life, as Paul says (Eph. 4), many will be rejected as unfit when the King says, "My friend, how did you get in here?"

All this the parable teaches and demonstrates clearly and precisely. But since preachers often allow themselves to be moved and driven by what their hearers want to hear, as it is written, Isa. 30, "Tell us pleasant things!" or as Paul writes in 2 Timothy 4, "They choose teachers according to their own desires, according to their itching ears;" and since the hearers likewise remain so firmly set in their chosen delusion that even on the Last Day many evildoers will say, "Lord, Lord, why should we be condemned? We, too, wish to be saved!" (Mat. 7), this parable has been given for a warning and admonition for both preachers and hearers. To the preachers, so that they discharge their office with faithful diligence and zeal, according to the instructions of the heavenly King, so that no one may lose his salvation. For if they do not invite the guests in the way that the King has prescribed, then they will carry themselves and the guests into eternal damnation. Therefore, they should call out confidently and raise their voice like a trumpet, proclaiming to the people their sin and their transgression (Isa. 58). They should reveal God's wrath from heaven (Rom. 1), even as the Lord Christ teaches the Jews their lesson in this parable. For God says in Ezekiel 3: "When I say to the sinner, 'You will surely die!' and you, preacher, whom I have made a watchman, do not point it out to the ungodly, then the ungodly will surely die in his sins, but I will demand his blood from your hands. But if you tell him, then you will have saved your soul." Indeed, the servant of this King must not consider whether he will be mistreated or killed for it. In the same way, since the servants are not to preach or say anything but what the King has prescribed for them, "All is ready!"—that is, how Christ, who is God and Man, is the wedding garment—a preacher must see to it that none of the leaven of false doctrine be mingled in with the Word and Sacraments. And if he perceives that this is happening, he must take action against the wolf and faithfully warn the lambs, not only in general, but wherever necessity demands, expressly and specifically, as, for example, when a new, false Calvinist catechism arises, whether it comes from the Palatinate or from Wittenberg.* Likewise, whoever teaches that it is not the obedience and merit of Christ alone, grasped by faith, that is necessary for our salvation, but also our good works, he must rebuke such teaching and warn against it. He must also earnestly reprove those who rely only on an outward appearance, without true repentance and amendment of

---

* At the time of the publication of this sermon, Wittenberg was under the influence of theologians with Calvinist leanings. The 1574 Diet of Torgau brought their influence to an end.

life, for otherwise he makes himself a participant in the sins of another and will be responsible for the condemnation of his hearers, since he did not warn them of their destruction according to his office.

The hearers in this parable also receive their own warning and admonition, distributed bit by bit, so that every false delusion is met. For example, when God's Word admonishes, "Repent! Stop it! Sorrow over your sin! Cling to the Word and Sacraments!," and you lift up your hard, impenitent head and either expressly say, together with the wicked (Jer. 44), "I will not!" or you in fact demonstrate with your security and impenitence that you belong among those of whom the parable says, "And they were not willing to come"—then they are idle, useless thoughts if you go on imagining, "But I have God's Word! Christ has died! I, too, will surely be saved, etc.!"

So keep reading in the parable, if you continually let our Lord God reprove, bid, and implore you in His Word, and you, for your part, continue to go forth without repentance, according to the lusts of your flesh. When our dear God invites you to Word and Sacrament, you despise the Word and use neither Absolution nor Sacrament, as we sadly see everywhere in this principality. A few years ago, under the rule of the papacy, there was great hunger and thirst for the true use of the Lord's Supper, as it was instituted by the Lord Christ. But now, when, by God's grace, our Lord Christ calls out everywhere, practically on a daily basis, "Come! Eat! Drink!," hardly anyone is to be found, and the Son of God often prepares His Table in vain and to no purpose. And here we should not think, "It matters not. We are still good Evangelicals. We have God's Word!" For it says, "Many are called, but few are chosen." We should surely understand nothing else but that these words are meant to ring in our ears, as the parable says, "The guests were not worthy," and, "the King was angry." Likewise, "Bind him hand and foot, etc."

But when someone mistreats, persecutes, or kills this King's servants on account of their reproving office or teaching office, the world has its own common saying: "What do I care what the priest has to say about it? The priests are always complaining, always trying to reform everything, etc." Now, if they were great secular rulers, then one might easily concede and say, "Against our Lord God I will undertake nothing. I will not reject His Word! But I will not suffer it from the priests, etc." But what, indeed, should our Lord God care when someone mistreats, persecutes and kills even a poor parish priest, as long as he says that he thinks highly of our Lord God and is a good Evangelical, etc.? But hear what this parable says. When some mistreated and killed His servants, the King became angry, sent out His army, killed these murderers and burned up their city. That is, such a sin is punished with God's wrath, and even with outward, temporal punishments, as it is written in 2 Chr. 36: "The Lord sent them His messengers early, for He had compassion on His people. But they mocked the messengers of God, despised their word, and scoffed at His prophets, until the wrath of the Lord awoke against His people, so that there was no more remedy, etc." And lest anyone begin to think that he is too mighty and is prepared for this, the examples old and new demonstrate that this judgment of God stands fast and always comes in the end. "The King sent His army out and killed those murderers and burned up their city, etc."

Finally, there is one man in this parable who does not say that he will not come. Nor does he mistreat and kill the servants of this King. Nor does he wish to be reputed as one who despises Word and Sacrament. On the contrary, he sits together at the table, devotes himself to the Word, prides himself in the Gospel, always carries the Word in his mouth, etc. But he is only wearing a Pharisee's clothing, not a wedding garment. Therefore the King says, "Throw him out into the outer darkness." But you say, "How should I understand this, that I may guard against it and learn if it is directed against me?" Answer: The Scripture explains this for us very clearly. Namely, if you do not put off the Old Man, but remain, persist, and go on impenitently in sin, like when you pride yourself greatly in the Gospel and yet remain in security, hatred, gluttony, and unchastity, you torment and grieve people, you are unmerciful, etc. —when you, like the Pharisees, brush your sheep's clothing ever so clean and take great pride in the Gospel, the King will say to you, "My friend, how did you get in here without setting aside that old, nasty, filthy garment of sin, security, and impenitence? That is no wedding garment! Throw him out of here!" The same thing happens with our companions after a wild night of drinking. They have their own saying: "May God forgive us for what we've done today. We'll do it again tomorrow, if God grants us the opportunity!" But this is the "absolution" that pertains to such repentance: "Throw him out into the outer darkness, where there will be weeping and gnashing of teeth!"

But there is still another Pharisee's coat here, when the work-saints come along with their outwardly beautiful life, with their own works and merits, and sit alongside everyone else at the table. Not that it is evil or wrong to do good works, for our Lord God seeks them from us. But when a person mingles his good works into the article of justification and salvation; when he wants to bring them before God's tribunal and relies on them for his justification and salvation; when he thus wants to appear before God wearing the garment of his own works and either puts his trust entirely in them or tries to sew a new patch on the old garment (Mat. 9), that is, if he wants to mingle some of his own works with the merit of the Lord Christ in the article of justification and salvation, although this sounds good to human reason, when the King comes in to view the guests, He will say, "My friend, how did you get in here? You're not wearing the wedding garment!" For there is only one form of attire that is permitted at this wedding, only one garment that avails for salvation, namely, when we, through Word and Sacraments, put on the Lord Jesus Christ by faith (Gal. 3). That is the only robe of righteousness, the only garment of salvation, as Isaiah calls it, which can stand before the King for eternal life at this wedding. Whoever does not bring this garment with him, no matter how else he may have adorned and decorated himself, will be told in the end, "You are not wearing the right wedding garment. To the outer darkness with you, where there will be weeping and gnashing of teeth!"

So it is that, piece by piece, everything has been laid out beautifully in this parable so that everyone—no matter what kind of false delusion he is trapped in—finds a reproof, a warning, and an admonition. And we should also use it for our own correction, marking well that, even though temporal punishment may not always follow openly or immediately in this life (as the parable says, "He killed the murderers and burned up their city"), we should not therefore imagine that it is not coming, or that God is not angry. For most of His wrath is spared for the time when the King goes in to view His guests, that is, for the Last Day. Then He will also say to those who have been spared in this life, "To the outer darkness with you, where there will be weeping and gnashing of teeth!"

And yet, along with all of this there is also this great comfort: Although the guests despise it or say that they are not willing to come, the parable also says that "He again sent out other servants and said, 'Come to the wedding!'" That is, as the Epistle to the Hebrews says in chapter 3, "As long as it is still called 'Today,'" and the time of grace remains, the door is still open. But when the door closes, we will knock in vain (Mat. 25). For it says in Psalm 95 that He has sworn in His wrath, "They shall not enter His rest."

So then, let that summarize briefly and simply the second part of this parable—how each one should use it for reproof, warning, admonition, and correction. And the very fact that the Lord Christ warns the world so earnestly will serve as a witness upon it and against it.

Part 3

The following must also be shown alongside this doctrine of God's foreknowledge, namely, what a glorious, beautiful, dependable comfort is to be found in this doctrine for the poor, troubled, God-fearing consciences, and how they are to seek and find such comfort in this article. For, although this parable is primarily intended for the reproof, warning, and admonition of the Pharisees, it is set forth in such a way that the foundations of comfort can also be comprehended in a very lovely way. Since these are handled in other passages of Scripture more broadly and more clearly, we will, for brevity's sake, point out only the chief points, lest our sermon wax too long.

And this is the basis on which we shall begin, as the parable says, that the King sends His servants and ministers to call those whom He wants to have as guests at this wedding. That is, when I wonder and trouble myself about whether I, too, was foreseen for salvation, or whether I belong among the number of the elect, and whether my name, too, is written in the Book of Life—for no one else will be saved, except only the elect—I should not float between heaven and earth with uncertain, doubtful thoughts; or, as Paul says to the Romans in chapter 10, "ascend into heaven or go down into the deep." For about all such thoughts it says in Romans 11, "Who has known the mind of the Lord, or who has been His counselor?" Instead, I should seek this knowledge in the call, that is, in the Word of God which echoes in my ears and heart through the mouth of a man. There I can find it, as Paul says in Romans 10, "The Word is near you, in your mouth and in your heart." And in Eph. 1, "He has made known to us the mystery of His will, that it might be preached." Romans 8: "Those whom He foresaw or chose, them He also called." And that is a beautiful, glorious comfort, that I can know and learn through the call of the preached Word, what God concluded concerning me and my salvation before the foundation of the world was laid. Therefore Paul says in 1 Cor. 2, "We have known the mind of Christ, for God has revealed it to us by His Spirit." We can know how richly we have been graced by God, for when God calls us through the Word, we should not imagine, "Yes, He calls me through the Word, but who knows whether He also means it in His heart?" For the fact that He gladly wants me to be saved when He calls me through the Word—that is demonstrated by this parable, "and the King was angry when the invited guests were not willing to come." And the fact that He also means me in particular with the common invitation, that I know from this, that in the Absolution and in the Sacrament, the common promise is applied—indeed, sealed and proven—to me in particular. We should not think or judge differently about God's will toward us than what He has revealed in His Word. Indeed, he commits a great blasphemy who imagines that God reveals one thing to us through His

Word and actually thinks something else in His heart. For such a thing is punished even among men, when a person says one thing but means another (Psa. 12).

Now, it is certainly true that no one will be saved unless he receives the Word. It is also true that no one can receive the offered grace of God on his own, by his own strength. For whoever teaches that the natural free will of the unregenerate man has the power and ability to receive God's grace teaches against the entire Holy Scripture (1 Cor. 2, 2 Cor. 3, Rom. 8, etc.). But according to the Scripture, we cannot and should not judge differently from what God sets before us in His Word; namely, that it is His will to be effective in us by means of His Word and to work in us the ability to receive the offered grace by means of His gifts, strength, and working. But the natural wickedness of the flesh is surely also able to resist such divine working, and God surely knows and perceives beforehand which ones will do this. But I am not commanded to look into this. No, I think and judge according to God's Word, that when He calls me through the Word, He wants to work in me through it the strength to be able to receive it. And I pray my dear God that He, through His Spirit, might put to death the deeds of my flesh (Rom. 8); that I may not be found among those who resist His grace. For it is certainly true what is written in Hosea chapter 13: "Israel, you bring yourself to ruin. But your salvation is found only with Me."

Thus I have two beautiful bits of comfort from this doctrine. First, that I can have the certainty and assurance from the call that I, too, was foreseen and elected to salvation. Secondly, that I should have from the call a sure consolation that the Holy Spirit wants to work in me, through the Word, the strength and the ability to receive it.

And when I have this foundation, I can go back and confidently conclude that my salvation was so important to our Lord God that He planned it before the foundation of the world was laid. And since I was predestined for salvation already at that time, my salvation will surely be mightily preserved against the weakness of my flesh, against the attacks of the world, and against all the power and cunning of the gates of hell. I also know from this that God will surely not change His mind and will, for Paul says in Rom. 11: "The gifts and call of God cannot be altered." This article also gives me the comfort that my salvation does not depend on my works or worthiness, for this grace was given me in Christ Jesus before the time of the world, when I did not yet exist, as Paul deals with this topic in 2 Timothy 1. Paul also draws the following comfort from this fact in Romans 8: Whatever good or ill befalls a called Christian in this world, all of it must serve for the best, since God, in His counsel, ordained before the time of the world how He would lead and bring each one through cross and misfortune to eternal glory.

Paul also takes great comfort from this and finds encouragement and joy in it, which he expresses in Rom.

8: "What shall we say? If God is for us, who can be against us? Who will separate us from the love of God? For I am convinced that neither death nor life, neither present nor future is able to separate us from the love of God that is in Christ Jesus our Lord, etc."

And since we see that many of those who began well later end up falling tragically and shamefully, it is likewise a hard and troubling question, whether and how I may remain steadfast in the midst of such great weakness. For it is written, "He who remains steadfast to the end will be saved." But this article offers a truly comforting answer to those who are called through the Word according to God's purpose. In John 10 Christ says, "My sheep hear My voice, and they will never perish, and no one will snatch them from My hand." 1 Cor. 1: "He will confirm you to the end, for God is faithful, through whom you were called into the fellowship of His Son." Phi. 1: "I am confident that He who began the good work in you will also carry it on to completion for the day of Jesus Christ." 1 The. 5: "The God of peace sanctify you, that your spirit, soul and body be preserved irreproachable at the coming of Jesus Christ. He who calls you is faithful, and He will also do it." 1 Pet. 5: "The God of all grace, who has called us to His eternal glory in Christ Jesus, will perfect, strengthen, empower, and settle you." These beautiful, comforting passages base our perseverance on this: that He who called us to His glory through the Word is faithful. And even though we sometimes founder, fall, and do not immediately get back up when He calls us, this parable gives us beautiful comfort when it says that, "He again sent out other servants and said, 'Tell the guests, "Come to the wedding!"'"

In Part 1 it was also explained what great comfort is to be found in the fact that our salvation is described with this comparison of a King who made a wedding for His Son. And pious Christians can understand it in this way: In the beginning, before the Fall, God had bestowed on Adam all the gifts and properties of the pure, perfect human nature in such a way that, if he had remained steadfast, they would have been passed down from him to all his descendants. But Adam did poorly in preserving these goods for us. Therefore, in the redemption, God wanted to preserve our salvation in a better, firmer, surer manner. So He united the human nature with the divine in one person with His Son, so that our salvation should now be better preserved than it was in the first Adam.

It is also comforting that this King had His guests called out of all kinds of people and stations, especially when the parable says, "They brought together whomever they found, evil and good." In other words, no one is such a great sinner or so deeply fallen that he should be excluded from this wedding, if he is called and converted, for all is ready! Also, no one is so good and pious that he has no need of this wedding, where everything that is necessary for our justification before God and for our salvation is already prepared by grace, only through Christ.

Something was mentioned in Part 1 about the wedding garment. But that, too, presents a beautiful, glorious comfort. For Paul says in 2 Cor. 5 that we will be clothed with eternal glory, "if indeed, having been clothed, we shall not be found naked." But Job says in chapter 4, "Among His servants, none is without reproach, and in His angels He finds foolishness. How much more those who dwell in houses of clay, who are founded on earth!" And Isaiah complains in chapter 64, "All our righteousness is like an unclean garment." With what, then, are we to be clothed, so that we may stand approved at this wedding when the King comes in to view His guests? Psalm 45 says, "The bride stands in pure, precious gold; the King's daughter is dressed with golden articles. So the King will desire your beauty." But where shall we acquire such a beautiful garment that the King may be so pleased with it? And without a doubt it must surely be a beautiful garment—so pure that we will not be cast out into the outer darkness, where there is weeping and gnashing of teeth. The old, spotted robe of sins will not do. Paul writes to the Philippians about this in chapter 3, that even our righteousness is no different than filth and rubbish. But the Scripture shows us a single, holy adornment that can stand before this King for salvation, namely, Christ Jesus with the merit of His obedience, suffering and death, which we put on through faith, in Word and Sacraments (Gal. 3). That is what Psalm 45 means when it says, "The daughters of the King ride in your adornment." And Isaiah, in chapter 61: "My soul is joyful in my God, for He has clothed me with garments of salvation, and has dressed me with the robe of righteousness." Concerning this garment we ought not doubt, but be certain that, clothed in it, we will be acceptable to the King when He comes to view His guests, and will be pleasing to Him even unto eternal life. In addition, we certainly also put on the New Man (Eph. 4), who is "created in the image of God, in true righteousness and holiness." But since this renewal is not entirely pure and perfect, we neither can nor should bring it before God's tribunal. Instead, Christ alone, who has been made for us righteousness, sanctification, and redemption by God, should be our only wedding garment. And although we are despised in this world, we know for certain that, when the King comes in to view His guests, we, being dressed in this garment, will be truly well-pleasing to Him unto eternal life.

Thus we have dealt simply with this Gospel. First, we saw how the doctrine of God's foreknowledge is simply grasped in this parable. Secondly, we saw how we should use this doctrine as a warning, admonition, and correction. Thirdly, we noted how we may seek and find beautiful comfort in this doctrine. May our dear God give us His Holy Spirit, grace, and blessing, that we may thus always use it for instruction, correction, and comfort. Amen.

www.ingramcontent.com/pod-product-compliance
Lightning Source LLC
Chambersburg PA
CBHW070803050426
42452CB00012B/2472